31 Days of

Health, Wealth & Happiness

Health, Wealth & Happiness

Joshua Mills

31 DAYS OF HEALTH, WEALTH & HAPPINESS
Joshua Mills

© 2011 Joshua Mills

ISBN: 978-0-9830789-5-1

Published by New Wine International, Inc.
www.NewWineInternational.org

Cover design by Ken Vail of Prevail Creative, Charlottetown, PEI, Canada. PrevailCreative.com
Interior design by David Sluka

Printed in the United States of America

Dedication

*This book is dedicated
to my dear friend*

Dr. Kaye R. Beyer

Contents

Introduction

"Beloved, I pray that in all respects you may prosper and be in good health, just as your soul prospers."
3 John 1:2, NASB

It is my greatest prayer that as you read this book, you will allow the revelations from these principles to sink deep down into the core of your being. Just as John the Apostle prayed, I too eagerly desire to see you blessed, and that in your natural prosperity, your happiness, and your physical health you may be as prosperous as you are in your spiritual walk with the Lord.

The first part of this book contains three very important teachings: **8 Reasons Why Healing Belongs To You**, **3 Keys For Discovering Your Prosperity**, and **12 Golden**

Principles For Experiencing Happiness. These foundational teachings serve as a powerful tool for utilizing this book, *31 Days of Health, Wealth & Happiness*. As you read, allow the Holy Spirit to renew your mind and prepare your heart for 31 amazing days of wisdom and daily activations.

You can experience *Health, Wealth and Happiness* all the days of your life!

In His Great Love,
Joshua Mills

Before it begun
 You already won.

When He said "it is finished"
 Your problems diminished.

You now have the victory
 So rejoice in that Glory.

Jesus paid the great price
 For you to now live in Christ.

You can walk in divine
 Health, Wealth & Happiness.

8 Reasons Why Healing Belongs To You!

1. Healing Brings Glory To God!

People get excited when healings begin to happen. *In an atmosphere of healing you will discover an atmosphere of celebration!* Last year as I was ministering in Colombo, Sri Lanka, one young lady came seeking prayer for her eyes. She couldn't see very well and she had been dealing with a spirit of blindness. As I laid my hands on her eyes, the power of God touched her body, and suddenly without any strained effort of her own, she began seeing clearly! Without hesitation this young lady began shouting and rejoicing loudly as she was awakened to the operative healing power of the Holy Spirit! All throughout Scripture, we find a connection between healing miracles and people responding to that realm by giving praise and glory to God! *"Great crowds came to him, bringing the lame, the blind, the crippled, the mute and many others, and laid them at his feet; and he healed them. The people were amazed when they saw the mute speaking, the crippled made well, the lame walking and the blind seeing. And they praised the God of Israel."* (Matthew 15:30-31, see also Matthew 9:8; Acts 4:21)

2. Healing Declares That The Enemy Has Been Defeated!

The work of the enemy is sickness, disease, and infirmity. The enemy brings pain and suffering. Jesus Christ came to give you a better way to live. While the enemy comes to steal, kill, and destroy, Jesus gives life more abundantly. Healing declares that the enemy has been defeated because it testifies to God's overcoming power and strength in your life! Healing belongs to you! *"He who does what is sinful is of the devil, because the devil has been sinning from the beginning. The reason the Son of God appeared was to destroy the devil's work."* (1 John 3:8, see also Acts 10:37-38)

3.   Healing Confirms The Word Of God!

Healing is a sign. The Scriptures tell us that healing is a sign that confirms the truth. It is a sign of God's love for you. It is an outward sign of an inner work. *If you choose to live in the truth, then nothing that the enemy has ever said about you can prosper.* You do not need to be sick. Through salvation in Jesus Christ, you have been freed from the curse of sin and death (Romans 6:22; Galatians 3:13). The Word of God is living and active, healing and restorative. *Wherever the Word is preached, healing can be reached* because healing confirms the Word of God. *"Then the disciples went out and preached everywhere, and the Lord worked with them and con-*

firmed his word by the signs that accompa-nied it." (Mark 16:20, see also John 10:37-38)

4. Healing Fulfills God's Promise To You!

The Word of God declares that you have been healed by the stripes that Jesus Christ bore on his back. It is a promise. In order to receive this promise, you must first believe it and then simply receive it. If Jesus Christ paid for it, then it's a done deal and it belongs to you. *Trust God's promises. Rest in God's promises. Receive God's promises.* As a promise, healing belongs to you! *"When evening came, many who were demon-possessed were brought to him, and he drove out the spirits with a word and healed all the sick. This was to fulfill what was spoken through the prophet Isaiah: 'He took up our infirmities and carried our diseases.'"* (Matthew 8:16-17, see also Mark 7:27-28)

5. Healing Releases Joy!

Sickness brings pain and misery, but healing releases joy! There is a very special connection between the two because joy also releases healing! When joy begins to rise up on the inside of you, you're gaining power over the enemy's tactics because *"...the joy of the Lord is your strength"* (Nehemiah 8:10). The Word of God also tells us that laughter is just as good as a medicine (Proverbs 17:22).

I recently read an interesting newspaper article explaining that the University of California in Los Angeles is now starting a laughter program for hospital patients stricken by cancer and other diseases. The scientific world has examined humor and has discovered that laughter has an effect on most of the major physiological systems of the body. Lab experimentation has demonstrated these positive effects on the respiratory, cardiovascular, and immune systems.

The Word of God becomes very much alive in the light of these new studies. Joy releases healing, and healing releases great joy! *"Philip went down to a city in Samaria and proclaimed the Christ there. When the crowds heard Philip and saw the miraculous signs he did, they all paid close attention to what he said. With shrieks, evil spirits came out of many, and many paralytics and cripples were healed. So there was great joy in that city."* (Acts8:5-8)

6. Healing Announces The Kingdom Of God!

When the supernatural power of God comes onto the scene with healing miracles and miraculous signs, it announces the kingdom of God and declares that Jesus Christ saves and heals all! *"Heal the sick who are there and tell them, 'The kingdom of God is near you.'"*(Luke 10:9) (see also Matthew 12:28)

7. Jesus Christ Heals All!

Healing is not reserved for a select few. When Jesus Christ was on the earth, He went about doing good and healing ALL people. When you invite Jesus Christ into your heart through a personal salvation experience, in essence, you invite the healing power of God to touch every area of your life – spirit, soul and body. *"How God anointed Jesus of Nazareth with the Holy Spirit and power, and how he went around doing good and healing all who were under the power of the devil, because God was with him."* (Acts 10:38)

8. Jesus Christ Paid For Your Healing!

Jesus Christ already paid for your healing in full. When He hung on the cross, He declared that "it is finished." Don't let the devil try to steal this healing from you. The enemy may attempt to give you symptoms of sickness or feelings of infirmities, but the Bible declares that Jesus Christ has already settled the deal by the stripes He bore on His back. Jesus Christ paid for your healing, so it belongs to you! *"He himself bore our sins in his body on the tree, so that we might die to sins and live for righteousness; by his wounds you have been healed."* (1 Peter 2:24)

Recommended Resources:

- *31 Days To A Miracle Mindset* – Book (#BK-11)

- *Healing For Your Body* – Ministry Card (#MC-05)

- *40 Healing Scriptures* – Ministry Card (#MC-06)

- *Intensified Glory Institute*® *Home Study Course* – DVD Set (#PK-09)

3 Keys For Discovering Your Prosperity

1. Consult God's Wisdom

The Word of God is the wisdom of God. *"Wisdom is supreme; therefore get wisdom. Though it cost all you have, get understanding"* (Proverbs 4:7). The spiritual principles and insight of God's Word will work for you if you will allow it to transform your attitude and outlook. Never make any important decisions, relocations, or major investments without first consulting the Holy Spirit. He is the Spirit of Wisdom, Knowledge, and Revelation (Colossians 2:2-3). If you follow the leading of the Holy Spirit in your personal and business matters, you will begin discovering the abundant blessings that

21

overtake the *Obedient*. *"He who gets wisdom loves his own soul; he who cherishes understanding prospers"* (Proverbs 19:8). God's wisdom brings clarity, creates peace, and produces good fruit. Wisdom will guide you to places of treasure that no one else has yet uncovered. *"But the wisdom that comes from heaven is first of all pure; then peace-loving, considerate, submissive, full of mercy and good fruit, impartial and sincere."* (James 3:17)

2.   Make Wise Investments

Everything God has ever given to you has been deposited as a seed into your life. *"For God is the one who provides seed for the farmer and then bread to eat. In the same way, he will provide and increase your resources and then produce a great harvest of generosity in you"* (2 Corinthians 9:10, NLT). Your time is a seed. Your talents and abilities are a seed. Your love and compassion toward others is a seed. Your testimony is a seed. Your finances are a seed. What will you do with these seeds? *A seed is created to be invested, not to be ingested.* The potential of the seed will never be known until it has been planted into the fertile soil of opportunity. It's very important to realize that the potential for harvest in your life is continually surrounding you. You must discern your seeds and discern your soil. What people, places, ideas, or moments has God given to you as fertile soil for your seeds?

When I was twenty-one years old, a mentor told me something I will never forget. He said, *"Never stay where you're tolerated; find the place where you're celebrated."* Do not sow your seeds into hard ground. Do not invest into thorny places or ungrateful people because it will choke your seed and cause your dreams to die quickly. Find the soil that's ready to receive your precious seeds and make your investments wisely. Also, do not sow into only one field. The Bible instructs you to scatter your seed, so spread it out and receive a return from many sources. You never know which one may prosper most. *"Sow your seed in the morning, and at evening let not your hands be idle, for you do not know which will succeed, whether this or that, or whether both will do equally well."* (Ecclesiastes 11:6)

3.   Receive Your Returns

Every investment will bring a return. This is a spiritual principle. *"Don't be misled—you cannot mock the justice of God. You will always harvest what you plant"* (Galatians 6:7, NLT). If you invest poorly, you will receive a return of sorrows. But if you invest wisely, you will receive a return of prosperity. Do not ignore your returns. Learn from your mistakes and focus on your victories!

When you've consulted God's wisdom for instruction and you've been led by the Spirit to invest properly, do not "feel guilty" about receiving the good benefits of your wise investments. Luke 6:38 tells us that there are seven supernatural levels for receiving (I have an entire teaching on this in my profound book *Positioned For Prosperity*). Just as you have learned how to be a generous investor, you must also learn how to be a generous receiver.

A few years ago the Lord showed me that after a person has broken through a poverty spirit in the area of their giving, often this poverty spirit tries to defeat them in their ability to receive. A religious spirit will make you feel bad about receiving nice gifts or generous amounts of blessing. The Bible tells us that the sole reason why God blesses His people is not to make them greedy, but He blesses them in order to enable them to be a blessing for others! *You can only give away what you possess.* This is why God wants to bless you with good things while you're here on the earth.

You have an assignment to the poor and the hurting (James 1:27). You are chosen of the Lord to proclaim the salvation of God and to release freedom for the captives (Isaiah 61:1-3). You must break through in your ability to receive! Recognize the harvest. Discern your blessings. Receive them and utilize them as another investment for the flow of unlimited miracles!

Recommended Resources:

- *Positioned For Prosperity* – Book (#BK-15)
- *Miracle Money* – Teaching CD (#CD-14)
- *Kingdom Economics In The Glory Realm* – Ministry Card (#MC-13)
- *Proverbs Of Prosperity* – Ministry Card (#MC-14)
- *7 Keys For Living In Abundance* – Ministry Card (#MC-15)

12 Golden Principles For Experiencing Happiness

1. Trust In The Lord

You will never experience true happiness until you can trust in Jesus Christ (if you don't know Him yet, turn to the Prayer To Receive Salvation page after Day 31 at the back of this book). When all else fails, he remains faithful and true. Trust His Word because it works (Hebrews 4:12). Trust His love because it's never deficient in compassion (1 Corinthians 13:8). Trust His Spirit because He is all-powerful and well able to work a miracle for you (Romans 8:11). *"O taste and see that the Lord [our God] is good! Blessed (happy, fortunate, to be envied) is the man*

27

who trusts and takes refuge in Him." (Psalm 34:8, AMP)

2. Embrace God's Peace

Most often you are your worst critic. Don't be so hard on yourself anymore. Accept Christ's peace and forgiveness, which allow you to experience the happiness that God provides. Saint Francis De Sales said, *"Have patience with all things, but chiefly have patience with yourself. Do not lose courage in considering your own imperfections, but instantly set about remedying them – every day begin the task anew."* **"And the peace of God, which transcends all understanding, will guard your hearts and your minds in Christ Jesus."** (Philippians 4:7)

3. Remain Thankful

If you're foolish, then you'll count your problems. But if you're wise, then you'll count your blessings! Thankfulness is one of the keys to contentment. It is the key to divine health and it is the key for extraordinary opportunities. *Gratitude is the key for opening the door to more.* The fullness of God's miraculous presence can only be experienced by a thankful heart. It is even more important to *express it* than only just to *feel it*. The famous preacher William Arthur Ward said, *"Feeling gratitude and not expressing it is like wrapping a present and not giving it."* Show your thankfulness by writing an email, making a phone call, or by reaching out to comfort those who have comforted you. **"Enter into His gates with thanksgiving and a thank offering and into His courts with praise! Be thankful and say so to Him, bless and affectionately praise His name! For the Lord is good; His mercy and loving-kindness are everlasting, His faithfulness and truth endure to all generations."** (Psalm 100:4-5, AMP)

4. Rejoice In The Lord Always

Rejoicing in the Lord positions you for the victory. The enemy has been defeated. In the spiritual realm your problems have already been overcome. When you learn how to praise during the midnight difficulties, it won't be very long until the blessings of morning come! This is something that you must purpose to do. Declaring the victory will cause you to feel different about your situation. Remember that no weapon that's been formed against you will prosper (Isaiah 54:17). Hang on... keep going... don't lose faith. A promise is a promise. God is faithful to fulfill His Word for you (1 Corinthians 1:9). You can rejoice in Him. *"Always be full of joy in the Lord. I say it again—rejoice!"* (Philippians 4:4, NLT)

5. Spend Time In God's Presence

In the presence of the Lord there is joy forevermore (Psalm 16:11). In God's presence you are touched by His life. In His presence you are healed by His light. In His presence you are counseled by His wisdom. In His presence you are comforted by His voice. In His presence your problems disappear as the brilliance of His glory shines on you. In His presence you are forever transformed and changed. Discover the wonderful benefits of encountering God's presence on a daily basis and you will experience new found happiness. *"There, in the presence of the LORD your God, you and your families shall eat and shall rejoice in everything you have put your hand to, because the LORD your God has blessed you."* (Deuteronomy 12:7)

6. Stay Teachable

Nothing will hinder you more than arrogance. The Scriptures declare that, *"Pride goes before destruction, a haughty spirit before a fall"* (Proverbs 16:18). It is important to stay teachable in order to fulfill your assignment on the earth. God will send you teachers, mentors, and instructors who carry revelation that you need in order to be successful. It's important to honor these men and women that God assigns to your life. Allow them to speak, educate, correct, or re-align areas where they see you need an adjustment. You can glean from their wisdom and learn from their mistakes.

My life and ministry is indebted to the amazing mentors that I have had. Before I entered into full-time traveling ministry on my own, I spent the first five years traveling with other Pastors and Evangelists. I served them, honored them, and learned how to be obedient to their instructions. *"Happy and fortunate is the man whom God reproves; so do not despise or reject the correction of the Almighty [subjecting you to trial and suffering]."* (Job 5:17, AMP)

7. Be Diligent At Your Job

The Scriptures give us an understanding that hard work pays off. Hard work is one key to success that can never be underestimated! Your employment is not just for financial gain; it is also an investment of your time that reflects your attitude, abilities, ethics, and morale. Recognize that God has given you a job for a specific reason and He will reward you as you work with excellence. Your job is your ministry assignment. Do not slack on your assignment. Stay focused, accomplished, and determined to do everything as unto the Lord. *"For the LORD your God will bless you in all your harvest and in all the work of your hands, and your joy will be complete."* (Deuteronomy 16:15)

8. Learn How To Walk In God's Love And Forgiveness

When you walk in God's love, then you walk in His power. Love is patient, kind, forgives and covers all wrongs; it exchanges despair for contentment and happiness (Ephesians 4:32). Thomas Chalmers said, *"Unforgiveness is the poison we drink hoping another will die."* One of the greatest things you can learn to do is to walk in God's love and forgiveness.

Lewis B. Smedes has been quoted as saying, *"Forgiving does not erase the bitter past. A healed memory is not a deleted memory. Instead, forgiving what we cannot forget creates a new way to remember. We change the memory of our past into a hope for our future."* When you learn how to walk in forgiveness and love, you discover new possibilities for happiness to abound in your life. Love God and love others. **"Blessed (happy, fortunate, to be envied) is he who has forgiveness of his transgression continually exercised upon him, whose sin is covered."** (Psalm 32:1)

9. Pursue Healthy Relationships

Often the troubles you face in life can be attributed to the friends and relationships that you have chosen to develop. It has been said that misery enjoys company. Abusive relationships will create abusive situations, while loving relationships will create loving situations. It is very important for you to develop healthy, loving, and Christ-centered relationships that will encourage you toward being your best. Do not spend time with others who do not recognize God's potential inside of you. Learn how to appreciate your family members and celebrate their strengths. Fellowship with believers who discern your talents, your abilities, and those who will challenge you to be who God has called you to be! *"Blessed (happy, fortunate, prosperous, and enviable) is the man who walks and lives not in the counsel of the ungodly [following their advice, their plans and purposes], nor stands [submissive and inactive] in the path where sinners walk, nor sits down [to relax and rest] where the scornful [and the mockers] gather."* (Psalm 1:1, AMP)

10. Create An Atmosphere For Rest And Relaxation

After you've taken care of your daily duties and assignments, create an atmosphere for rest and relaxation. This could be at the end of your day before retiring to bed, or even during set hours on the weekend. It's necessary to schedule this time into your agenda. In order to work at your fullest potential, it's very important to make time for rest. God rested on the seventh day of creation as an example for us all (Genesis 2:2).

One way you can create an atmosphere for relaxation is by taking a calming, warm bath before going to bed. Relaxing in the bathtub helps to relieve tense muscles and can also aid in re-energizing your body from feeling exhausted or stressed by daily pressures, aches, and pains. While you're enjoying your bath, you could also consider playing gentle *SpiritSpa* music in the background or dimming the lights. Another way to relax is by utilizing the calming benefits of massage. I personally enjoy receiving a foot massage after days of standing on my feet while preaching for hours. It helps greatly in restoring my ability to stand for long hours. I also enjoy giving Janet Angela a scalp massage that will prepare her for a good night's rest. While I'm giving her this massage, I can also use this time to pray for her and release God's blessings to her.

During their healing rituals, the Old Testament priests would often touch specific points of a person's body, anointing their hands or feet (Leviticus 14:17). This is very interesting as recent medical studies have confirmed specific emotional release points within those parts of the body. *"Therefore, since the promise of entering his rest still stands, let us be careful that none of you be found to have fallen short of it."* (Hebrews 4:1)

11. Always Choose Integrity

Shortly before Dr. Oral Roberts passed away, Janet Angela and I had a special opportunity to sit at his feet one afternoon as we gathered together in his living room in Newport Beach, California. He was such a great man of faith, a real General in God's

Army. He personally witnessed hundreds of thousands of people being healed in his tent revivals and he went on in life to do something that others thought was impossible: he built a world-renowned university and a hospital where faith and miracles happened on a daily basis.

But the thing that struck me the most about Dr. Oral Roberts that afternoon wasn't the miracles he had seen or other great accomplishments. It was the fact that he had lived his life with integrity. Ruth Ward Heflin once said, *"The anointing is God's gift to mankind, but integrity is our gift back to God."* When you choose to walk in honor, dignity, and integrity, you are leaving a tremendous legacy for others to follow in your footsteps. It's not how you start the race, but how you finish it that counts. Choosing to do the right thing and walking in integrity will position you for untold happiness – knowing that you've always done the right thing! ***"Blessed (happy, fortunate, to be envied) is the man to*** *whom the Lord imputes no iniquity and in whose spirit there is no deceit."* (Psalm 32:2)

12. Give Generously To Others

Your life will never truly be enriched until you learn how to reach out unto others. As you give to others, it will come back to you. Many different cultures around the world recognize this spiritual principle. The Word of God calls it "sowing and reaping" (Galatians 6:9). Dr. Leo Buscaglia said, *"Too often we underestimate the power of a touch, a smile, a kind word, a listening ear, an honest compliment, or the smallest act of caring, all of which have the potential to turn a life around."* Learning how to be generous with your time, love, consideration, and finances will cause you to be a blessing to others and in turn you will also experience new dimensions of happiness in your own life. **"Blessed (happy, fortunate, to be envied) is he who considers the weak and the poor; the Lord will deliver him in the time of evil and trouble."** (Psalm 41:1, AMP)

Recommended Resources:

- *Atmosphere* – Book (#BK-17)
- *SpiritSpa* – Music CD (#CD-11)
- *I Am Blessed* – Ministry Card (#MC-11)
- *Giving Thanks* – Ministry Card (#MC-16)

Health, Wealth
& Happiness

Medicate on the Word of God.
It will strengthen your spirit,
soul, and body.

PROVERBS 4:20-22—My son, pay attention to what I say; listen closely to my words. Do not let them out of your sight, keep them within your heart; for they are life to those who find them and health to a man's whole body.

HEBREWS 4:12—For the word of God is living and active. Sharper than any double-edged sword, it penetrates even to dividing soul and spirit, joints and marrow; it judges the thoughts and attitudes of the heart.

Daily Activation

Research the following Scriptures in your Bible, write them down, and begin to declare them over your life. **Exodus 15:26; Psalm 103:1-5; Psalm 118:17; Jeremiah 30:17; Malachi 4:2; Mark 11:22-24; James 5:13-16.**

Generosity creates a realm for possibility. Giving is simply faith in action, reaching to receive the benefits of benevolence. Generosity is the activation for supernatural multiplication.

PROVERBS 19:17—He who is kind to the poor lends to the LORD, and he will reward him for what he has done.

MATTHEW 25:40—"The King will reply, 'I tell you the truth, whatever you did for one of the least of these brothers of mine, you did for me.'"

Daily Activation

Take a small step towards generosity today by giving something meaningful to someone else. You might want to bless somebody with a cup of coffee at the coffee shop today, or you could give away a special article of clothing to someone you know. Watch how God uses this simple action to bring blessings to many.

Happiness is... knowing that you're loved by God. His love is unfailing, unchanging, always reaching, and contains the power for miracles. Where there is great love there is always great miracles!

1JOHN 4:16-19—And so we know and rely on the love God has for us. God is love. Whoever lives in love lives in God, and God in him. In this way, love is made complete among us so that we will have confidence on the day of judgment, because in this world we are like him. There is no fear in love. But perfect love drives out fear, because fear has to do with punishment. The one who fears is not made perfect in love. We love because he first loved us.

Daily Activation

Today I want to challenge you to make a list of five different ways that you can better show love in order to experience the miracle that love creates. This could mean taking a special gift to an unfriendly neighbor, speaking kind words to a distant relative, or any number of other wonderful ideas. Be creative and discover the miracle of God's love in action!

Day 4

Your healing is more than a feeling. It comes from the finished work of Calvary. It's forever been settled in heaven, so receive this precious gift and allow it to be settled on the earth through you.

JOEL 3:10 (KJV)—Let the weak say, I am strong.

Daily Activation

I want you to start something today that will promote health within your physical body. I want you to drink more water! Your body needs water in order to regulate your body temperature, to transport oxygen to your cells, and to provide the means for nutrients to flow to all of your organs. Doctors suggest that you drink at least eight glasses of water per day. Drinking more water can also aid in weight-loss if necessary. If you want to make your water taste better, you can add a handful of frozen berries, slices of lemon, lime, or cucumber in your water bottle. Or try making natural herbal ice tea.

Day 5

You will never complain about the place that God has called you to once you recognize that it is always the place of blessing.

DEUTERONOMY 28:2-8—All these blessings will come upon you and accompany you if you obey the LORD your God: You will be blessed in the city and blessed in the country. The fruit of your womb will be blessed, and the crops of your land and the young of your livestock—the calves of your herds and the lambs of your flocks. Your basket and your kneading trough will be blessed. You will be blessed when you come in and blessed when you go out. The LORD will grant that the enemies who rise up against you will be defeated before you. They will come at you from one direction but flee from you in seven. The LORD will send a blessing on your barns and on everything you put your hand to. The LORD your God will bless you in the land he is giving you.

Daily Activation

Today make a list of five reasons why you're thankful. Use this list in your prayers this week, thanking the Lord for His goodness and His blessings that fill your life.

Day 6

Happiness is... experiencing joy in the middle of the night. Knowing that God's light outshines the darkness and His victories triumph over your troubles.

PSALM 134:1—Praise the LORD, all you servants of the LORD who minister by night in the house of the LORD.

Daily Activation

Every time something happens or somebody says something to you today that looks like bad news, I want you to celebrate the Lord with praise! You can respond to the situation by saying, *"Hallelujah!"* because your praise is bigger than your problem!

When you beg God for a healing, it displays your arrogance in believing that you have more compassion over the sickness than God does. The sacrifice of Jesus Christ is proof of God's desire for humanity to be healed. Now it's up to you to reach that ultimate conclusion. Thank God for your healing, praise Him for it, and rest in the peace of God knowing that He has already provided it.

ISAIAH 53:4-5—Surely he took up our infirmities and carried our sorrows, yet we considered him stricken by God, smitten by him, and afflicted. But he was pierced for our transgressions, he was crushed for our iniquities; the punishment that brought us peace was upon him, and by his wounds we are healed.

Daily Activation

Get a goodnight's sleep tonight. Go to bed earlier than usual and spend the first few minutes in bed reading healing Scriptures from the Word of God. After a goodnight's rest, you will feel energized and ready to wake up in the morning. It's true that *"the early bird gets the worm!"*

Day 8

Praise past your current condition in order to receive a miracle transition. You've got to do something you've never done before in order to get results that you've never had before!

JOSHUA 6:2-5—Then the LORD said to Joshua, "See, I have delivered Jericho into your hands, along with its king and its fighting men. March around the city once with all the armed men. Do this for six days. Have seven priests carry trumpets of rams' horns in front of the ark. On the seventh day, march around the city seven times, with the priests blowing the trumpets. When you hear them sound a long blast on the trumpets, have all the people give a loud shout; then the wall of the city will collapse and the people will go up, every man straight in."

Daily Activation

Take a step towards a miracle today by doing something that you've never done before. This will require that you step out of your comfort zone, whatever that may be... paint a picture, write a poem, learn a new word, or join a local health and fitness club.

Day 9

Happiness is... sensing God's peace inside when the storms of life rage on the outside. Just rest in the shelter of the Secret Place, securely hidden from all danger and fear.

MATTHEW 6:6—But when you pray, go into your room, close the door and pray to your Father, who is unseen. Then your Father, who sees what is done in secret, will reward you.

Daily Activation

I want you to discover the Secret Place today. Make an appointment to be with God. Set time aside from your busy schedule to commune with Him specifically through a time of worship, prayer, reading your Bible, and just spending time in His presence listening for His still, small voice. Find a secluded and private place where you can go and be with Him today.

Never stop believing for a miracle because God is always able to work one for you. Sometimes we don't understand the ways or times in which they come, but press in, hang on, and don't let go.

HEBREWS 10:36—You need to persevere so that when you have done the will of God, you will receive what he has promised.

Daily Activation

Stay positive. Successful people stayed focused on the possibilities instead of dwelling on the potential for failure. Dr. Robert H. Schuller has famously said *"When faced with a mountain I will not quit! I will keep on striv-*

ing until I climb over, find a pass through, tunnel underneath or simply stay and turn the mountain into a gold mine, with God's help!" Observe your own thoughts today and keep them in check with God's Word.

Day 11

There is nothing in life that you need that God has not already desired for you to have.

2 PETER 1:3—His divine power has given us everything we need for life and godliness through our knowledge of him who called us by his own glory and goodness.

Daily Activation

Today become content in the realization that you have everything you will ever need (Philippians 4:19). Reach out to others today by asking yourself the question, "How can I be a blessing today?" How can you make a generous contribution to your friends, family, and community starting today? Possibly you could share your talents, abilities, resources, or special connections with some-one else. It is only by spending yourself that you truly realize how rich you are in Christ!

Day 12

Healing begins within and then overflows without. Wherever God is present, His healing power is resident. Become a generous receiver so that you can be a generous releaser.

JEREMIAH 30:17—"But I will restore you to health and heal your wounds," declares the LORD.

Daily Activation

It's been said that *"hurt people, hurt people."* Today offer your feelings of pain, sickness, and inferiority to the Lord. Jesus Christ took care of your hurt over 2000 years ago as he went to the cross of Calvary (Isaiah 53:4-5). Receive God's love. Receive God's healing. Allow the Holy Spirit to give you supernatural solutions and victory over your hurts.

Day 13

God's initial idea was never healing. God's original intention for mankind was always divine health and wholeness, simply living in the grace of God that contains the power to keep you through every season of life.

ECCLESIASTES 3:1—There is a time for everything, and a season for every activity under heaven.

Daily Activation

Take a step toward living healthy this week. Today choose to snack on a few carrot sticks, a handful of fresh berries, or an apple instead of your favorite carb-filled munchies. These small steps toward a healthy lifestyle can result in big changes. They say, *"An apple a day keeps the doctor away!"*

Day 14

Those who are generous increase their capacity to receive. For those who withhold, their ability to maintain becomes smaller. Your seed was created to be invested not ingested.

HOSEA 10:12—Sow for yourselves righteousness, reap the fruit of unfailing love, and break up your unplowed ground; for it is time to seek the LORD, until he comes and showers righteousness on you.

Daily Activation

Go through your wardrobe today and pick out clothes that you haven't worn in a while. Find a special person or local charity that will accept your donation. *You must make room in order to receive the increase!*

Day 15

*Happiness is... showing generosity
toward those who are less fortunate
than you. Bless others with the
blessings you have received.*

TITUS 1:8—Rather he must be hospitable, one who loves what is good, who is self-controlled, upright, holy and disciplined.

Daily Activation

Invite someone to your house for a special meal, or prepare a baked treat or some other kind of dessert for someone else. You will be amazed to find out how much blessing this brings!

Day 16

Choose your words carefully because they are seeds that will grow a harvest! Do not be surprised by the results they provide. You will reap according to whatever you sow!

PROVERBS 25:11—A word aptly spoken is like apples of gold in settings of silver.

Daily Activation

Write a word of encouragement to someone today who has impacted your life in a powerful way—especially someone who may not realize it. This may be a new source of inspiration for them!

It's possible to count the seeds within an apple, but it's impossible to count the apples within an apple seed. Your seed contains the potential for unlimited blessing. Invest your seed and watch it grow!

2 CORINTHIANS 9:10—Now he who supplies seed to the sower and bread for food will also supply and increase your store of seed and will enlarge the harvest of your righteousness.

Daily Activation

Speak words of wisdom into someone's life today. Invest your wisdom as a seed into someone who is ready to receive it… and watch it grow!

Day 18

Happiness is... reconnecting with special friends and relationships that allow you to be yourself and encourage you toward your fullest potential.

PROVERBS 27:9—Perfume and incense bring joy to the heart, and the pleasantness of one's friend springs from his earnest counsel.

Daily Activation

Make an appointment with someone today to go for an afternoon coffee or lunch break where you can fellowship together and enjoy each other's company.

Day 19

The ability to participate in the miraculous only happens when you open up your mind to the unlimited potential of God's Spirit.

MARK 10:27—Jesus looked at them and said, "With man this is impossible, but not with God; all things are possible with God."

Daily Activation

Read a "miracle encounter" in the Bible today. Anyplace where Jesus did miracles in the New Testament is a great place to start (e.g., John 2). Let God speak to you through it, and look for opportunities to put your faith into action.

Happiness is... believing the
promises of God's Word,
knowing that when He said it,
He really meant it!

2 CORINTHIANS 1:20—For no matter how many promises God has made, they are "Yes" in Christ. And so through him the "Amen" is spoken by us to the glory of God.

Daily Activation

Read a promise from the Word of God to-day that relates to a current situation that you're facing. If you're dealing with loneliness, find a promise from God's Word about "comfort." If you're dealing with feelings of depression, find a promise from God's Word about "joy."

A miracle seed sown into miracle soil will always produce a miracle harvest! Embrace your harvest by releasing your seed.

PSALM 107:37—They sowed fields and planted vineyards that yielded a fruitful harvest.

GALATIANS 6:9—Let us not become weary in doing good, for at the proper time we will reap a harvest if we do not give up.

Daily Activation

Look for an opportunity to share the love of Jesus Christ with someone today. Let them know that there are only two kinds of people: those who are saved and those who are about to be!

Day 22

Praise looks good on you. It will change your appearance. It will change your outlook on life, and the way that others perceive you as well. Declaring the victory will accelerate you into freedom and liberty.

ISAIAH 61:1-3—The Spirit of the Sovereign LORD is on me, because the LORD has anointed me to preach good news to the poor. He has sent me to bind up the brokenhearted, to proclaim freedom for the captives and release from darkness for the prisoners, to proclaim the year of the LORD's favor and the day of vengeance of our God, to comfort all who mourn, and provide for those who grieve in Zion—to bestow on them a crown of beauty instead of ashes, the oil of gladness instead of mourning, and a garment of praise instead of a spirit of despair.

Daily Activation

Try writing a praise song today! You might feel stretched while you're doing this. Just simply put your feelings toward God on paper. Your words don't need to necessarily rhyme. Once you write it down, then it's time to practice singing it (you can do this in private if you want!). God loves the sound of your praise.

Day 23

Happiness is... enjoying every moment of life; celebrating the people, places, and opportunities that God has blessed you with; and focusing on heaven's possibilities instead of your earthly difficulties.

ZECHARIAH 4:6—So he said to me, "This is the word of the LORD to Zerubbabel: 'Not by might nor by power, but by my Spirit,' says the LORD Almighty."

Daily Activation

Dream big today. Heaven is the limit! Don't put any restrictions on what God can or cannot do with you. Spend this day "catching a vision" from the Lord.

Day 24

Allow the victory on the inside of you to overcome the defeat that surrounds you.

1 CORINTHIANS 15:57-58—Thanks be to God! He gives us the victory through our Lord Jesus Christ. Therefore, my dear brothers, stand firm. Let nothing move you. Always give yourselves fully to the work of the Lord, because you know that your labor in the Lord is not in vain.

2 CORINTHIANS 2:14-15—Thanks be to God, who always leads us in triumphal procession in Christ and through us spreads everywhere the fragrance of the knowledge of him. For we are to God the aroma of Christ among those who are being saved and those who are perishing.

Daily Activation

Fill your home with the sound of praise and worship today! Pick out your favorite CD and turn up the volume! *A voice of praise is a voice of victory!*

Day 25

You are a divine connection! Your voice has the potential to speak a timely word. Your touch contains the power to release healing to the sick. Your compassion for others has the God-given ability to set the captives free. You are a divine connection for divine presence.

MARK 16:15, 17-18—He said to them, "Go into all the world and preach the good news to all creation. And these signs will accompany those who believe: In my name they will drive out demons; they will speak in new tongues; they will pick up snakes with their hands; and when they drink deadly poison, it will not hurt them at all; they will place their hands on sick people, and they will get well."

Daily Activation

Find a place where you can exercise your ministry calling and anointing. Do not allow others to stifle your potential. Find a mentor or leader who recognizes God's ability in you and believes in God's dream for you! Honor your leaders, honor your gifting, honor the Lord with your ability.

Day 26

*In order to receive anything from
God, you must first believe that He
truly wants you to have it.*

HEBREWS 11:6—And without faith it
is impossible to please God, because
anyone who comes to him must believe that
he exists and that he rewards those who ear-
nestly seek him.

PSALM 84:11—For the LORD God is a
sun and shield; the LORD bestows favor and honor; no good thing does he withhold from those whose walk is blameless.

Daily Activation

Research these following Scriptures in your Bible, write them down, and begin to declare them over your life. **Proverbs 10:22; Proverbs 13:11; Proverbs 22:9; 2 Corinthians 9:6-15; Ephesians 1:3; 3 John 1:2.**

Day 27

*When you give away whatever
you possess, you make a way for
whatever you've been promised!
God never leaves you or forsakes
you. When you feel like you're
under, you've still got a seed
filled with wonder.*

2CORINTHIANS **9:6**—Remember this: Whoever sows sparingly will also reap sparingly, and whoever sows generously will also reap generously.

Daily Activation

Experience the joy of giving today! Be the most generous, over-the-top, seed sowing, extravagant giver the world has ever seen! Sow words of kindness today. Sow special seeds of forgiveness. Sow your time and energy by investing into someone else's life. Sow praise into the heavens. Sow a financial sacrifice.

Day 28

Happiness is... beholding the beauty
of God's wonder-full creation—
a fresh snowfall in winter, the
delicate dew drops of spring, the
warm sunbeams of summer, and
the magnificent colors of fall.
It's just glimpse of the beauty of
the One who created it all.

JOB 7:17—What is man that you make so much of him, that you give him so much attention?

Daily Activation

Take a walk today. This could be a short stroll down your street or a hike through the forest. Deliberately notice God's creation. Concentrate on seeing details that you've never noticed before.

Day 29

If you embrace God's love, you will embrace success because His love never fails. God's love has a zero percent failure rate! Perfect love will dispel your fears and bring forth faith that works! Love more and you will fear less. When fear is absent, faith is able to function.

PROVERBS 17:9—He who covers over an offense promotes love, but whoever repeats the matter separates close friends.

Daily Activation

Today I want you to call a friend or family member that you haven't spoken to in a while and let them know that you love them. Love works wonders.

Day 30

*It takes money to make money.
Every seed reproduces after its
own kind. Make God-investments
and you will reap the rewards
of a God-return.*

DEUTERONOMY 8:18—But remember the LORD your God, for it is he who gives you the ability to produce wealth, and so confirms his covenant, which he swore to your forefathers, as it is today.

Daily Activation

Ask the Lord today to show you a person, place, or ministry where you can sow a financial seed. You may want to sow into a local missions organization, an evangelistic outreach, or into the life of a person whom God puts on your heart. *Do not delay in responding to what the Lord reveals!*

Happiness is... recognizing that you are fearfully and wonderfully made in the image of God, created to reflect His glory and radiate His brilliant light on the earth.

2CORINTHIANS 3:18—And we, who with unveiled faces all reflect the Lord's glory, are being transformed into his likeness with ever-increasing glory, which comes from the Lord, who is the Spirit.

Daily Activation

I want you to stand in front of your mirror today and make this declaration: *"I was created to reflect the Glory of God. I radiate with His light. I emanate His life. God's Word is hidden in my heart and His love flows to release miracles everywhere I go. I am blessed to be a blessing. Divine health belongs to me. Supernatural wealth belongs to me. Complete happiness belongs to me because I am a child of God."*

Prayer for Salvation

The Bible says:

> *That if you confess with your mouth, "Jesus is Lord," and believe in your heart that God raised him from the dead, you will be saved. For it is with your heart that you believe and are justified, and it is with your mouth that you confess and are saved.*
> —Romans 10:9-10

If you want to give your life to Christ, pray this with me right now:

> *Father, thank you for forgiving my sins. Jesus, come into my heart. Make me the kind of person You want me to be. Thank You for saving me. Amen.*

The Bible is very clear that *"everyone who calls on the name of the Lord will be saved"* (Romans 10:13). Welcome to the family of

God! Please use the contact information on the last page of this book to let us know that you have chosen to follow Christ.

Dear Friend,

I believe that you are a kingdom connection! God wants to use you to make a difference in the lives of thousands around the world. Do you believe that?

I would like to invite you to become a *Miracle Worker* with me, and help me take this supernatural message of Jesus Christ and His glory to the far corners of the earth.

Partnership is not simply giving of your finances; it is more. When you become a *Miracle Worker* with this ministry, you will become an integral member of the New Wine International outreach ministry team with special opportunities and privileges that will position you to have global impact.

A *"Miracle Worker"* is a person who agrees to:
1. Financially support the ministry of New Wine International (NWI)
2. Pray faithfully for Joshua & Janet Angela Mills and the NWI Ministry Team as they carry the message of Jesus Christ around the world.
3. Pray for those who will receive ministry through NWI ministry events and resources.

Partnership is not only what you can do to help me, but also what I can do to help you. Becoming a *Miracle Worker* with NWI provides a covenant agreement between you and me. By being a *Miracle Worker,* you will connect with the anointing and glory on this ministry as I send you monthly updates and revelatory teachings on the glory realm. You will receive my continued prayer for you and your family and you will be linked with the unique anointing that is on this ministry for unusual signs and wonders.

There are currently several ways to partner with NWI. I want you to decide the partnership level according to what the Lord has placed in your heart to do.

In His Great Love,

Joshua Mills

P.S. *Call my office today to become a partner or register online so that I can send you a special Miracle Worker Welcome Package filled with special benefits and information.*

Toll-Free: **1-866-60-NEW-WINE**
Online 24/7:
www.NewWineInternational.org
www.PartnersInPraise.com

Books by Joshua Mills

31 Days To A Miracle Mindset
31 Days Of Health, Wealth & Happiness
Advanced School Of Miracles
Atmosphere
Into His Presence – Praise & Worship Manual
Ministry Resources 101
Personal Ministry Prayer Manual
Positioned For Prosperity
School Of Miracles, Volume I
School Of Signs & Wonders, Course I
School Of Signs & Wonders, Course II
Simple Supernatural
Simple Supernatural Study Guide
Third Day Prayers
Time & Eternity

Available online 24/7 at:
www.NewWineInternational.org

Contact Information

To order more copies of
31 Days Of Health,
Wealth & Happiness,
please visit the online store at:
www.IntensifiedGlory.com
or call toll-free:
1-866-60-NEW-WINE
(1-866-606-3994)

We have excellent bulk/wholesale discount-
ed prices for bookstores and ministries.
Please contact office@intensifiedglory.com
for more information.